MOUNTAIN BIKING

IN THE

LAKE DISTRICT

by

Bryan James

1

First published in Great Britain in 1998 by Trailblazer Publishing (Scarborough)

ISBN   1 899004 25 4

Trailblazer Publishing (Scarborough)
Stoneways
South End
Burniston
Scarborough. YO13 0HP

MAPS
The maps in this book are not to scale and are for guidance only. They do not accurately portray the right of way. It is the readers responsibility not to stray from the right of way and it is strongly advised that you take the relevant Ordnance Survey map with you on the ride.

WARNING
Whilst every effort has been made for accuracy neither the publisher nor the author bear responsibility for the alteration, closure or portrayal of rights of way in this book. It is the readers responsibility not to invade private land or stray from the public right of way for cyclists. All routes in the book should be treated with respect and all precautions taken before setting out. Any person using information in this book does so at their own risk.

CONTENTS

THE SAWREY SLOGGER

*H*awkshead is worth exploring if you can spare the time. There is an inter esting church, the Beatrix Potter museum, a 17th century Town Hall and many fine old buildings in the village. There is refreshment available in cafes and pubs so it is best if you explore the village at the end of your ride. As well as being 'Beatrix Potter land' , another famous lakes person, William Words worth, went to school here.

Along the way refreshments are available at the Tower Bank Arms at Far Sawrey and if you feel that someone is watching you as you ride through the village it could be Mrs Tiggy-Winkle, for this is where Beatrix Potter lived and based many of her children's books.

This route can be merged with route two if you wish to make a longer ride across to Skelwith Bridge.

- - - o O o - - -

THE FACTS
Distance: 8 miles (14km)
Grading: Moderate
Off Road: 50%
Start/Grid Ref: Hawkshead, GR 352982
Maps: O.S. Outdoor Leisure 7
Grub Stops: The Tower Bank Arms at Near Sawrey.
Lots of choice in Hawkshead

- - - o O o - - -

YOUR ROUTE

*S*tart from the car park at Hawkshead and take the road to Near Sawrey. It is perhaps best to ride along the quieter road on the west side of Esthwaite Water. At Near Sawrey turn left onto a narrow road almost opposite the Tower Bank Arms Inn. Continue straight ahead through the farmyard then onto a bridleway at the sign. Continue on passing a bridleway sign to Claife Heights then keep straight on along a walled track with blue waymarks.

Continue along passing Moss Eccles Tarn as the track zig-zags its way up the hill on a well defined track and through a gate. Pass by more Tarns and

4

up a grassy hill to the trees. Enter the forest through a gate at the blue way-mark . Soon, take the interesting track on the left as waymarked with a blue arrow to a well signed crossway of tracks. Turn left as signed 'Bridleway to Hawkshead'. The track now bends about a bit and climbs to another signed crossing of tracks. Turn left here signed 'Bridleway to Hawkshead'.

Continue along the track through several gates and a confirmation sign guiding you towards Hawkshead. Take the left track where it splits and continue along to the road. At the road turn left through Colthouse to eventually join the B5285 to Hawkshead.

OH! A DRUNKEN DUCK TO BE!

*N*ot with all that mud! But you might be AS drunk as a duck if you linger too long at this hostelry! The Drunken Duck Inn changed its name from the Barngates Inn due to a rather amusing occurrence. The tale goes that beer was spilled outside the Inn one day and ducks being what they are slurped the lot. As is usual after a binge they passed out and were taken for dead. They were plucked and laid on the table in the kitchen of the Inn. When the kitchen staff returned to prepare them for the oven the naked ducks were staggering around the kitchen presumably looking for an Alka Seltzer! The staff knitted the ducks woolly coats to keep them warm then returned them to their natural habitat.

- - - o 0 o - - -

THE FACTS
Distance: 9½ miles (15km)
Grading: Almost easy
Off Road: 20%
Start/Grid Ref: Hawkshead, GR 352982
Maps: O.S. Outdoor Leisure 7
Grub Stops: Drunken Duck Inn

- - - o 0 o - - -

YOUR ROUTE

Start from the car park in Hawkshead. Turn left out of the park. In about a mile turn left at the sign for 'Gondola Steam Boat Pier'. In a few hundred yards turn right then right again at 'T' junction. Continue along to the small village of Knipe Fold. As you enter the village near a junction and opposite the entrance to the Berwick Lodge turn left uphill along a wide track signed 'Unsuitable for Motors'.

Enjoy this ride along the old byway, take care down the hills and watch out for loose stones. Tarn Hows is on your left after you have climbed over Limestone Hill and a little further along on the right is a Tarn. At the road turn right then in about a mile turn left to ride to Elterwater village. Go right in the village then right again onto the B5343. In a few hundred yards turn left onto a quiet road. Keep straight ahead at the first junction then right at the next two to enjoy a scenic ride past Loughrigg Tarn to Skelwith Bridge. Join the A593 for a few yards heading south over the River Brathay and at the corner turn left onto a quiet road.

Make for Skelwith Fold then head south to arrive at the Drunken Duck in about two miles. Sit outside and enjoy the view or inside if it is a poor day. After having eaten and drunk your fill head off to Hawkshead via Outgate to return to your transport.

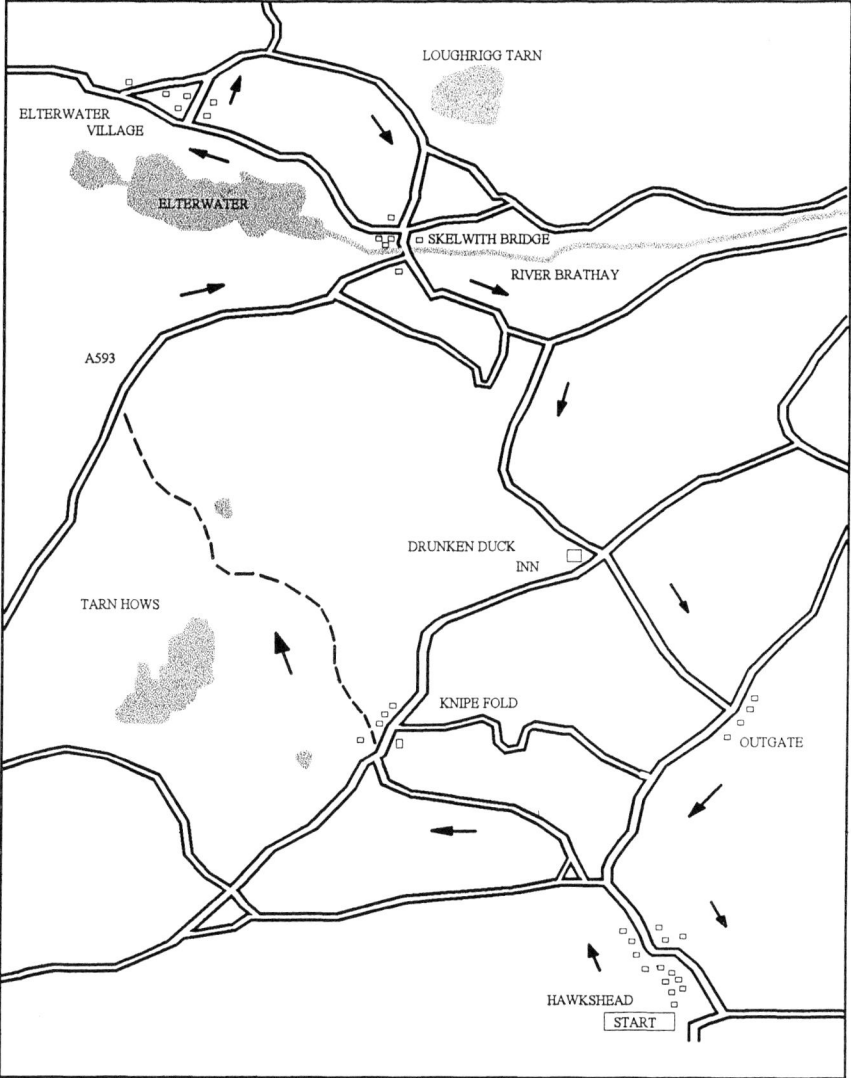

THE WATENDLATH WOBBLE

*T*his ride from Keswick is mainly on quiet roads, (if any roads in the Lake District can be called quiet!) The off road section is quite technical in places and is certainly not for the novice rider, although there is no problem if you were to dismount and walk the worst parts.

Borrowdale was inhabited by Cistercian monks in the 13th century and they gave the name to the village of Grange. This was probably where they had there farmstead. They were great sheep farmers obtaining most of their income from the wool trade.

The Bowderstone, a feature of Borrowdale, was transported by the great glaciers of the ice age. It stands 32 feet (10 metres) high, is 60 feet (18metres) long and weighs about 2000 tons.

--- o 0 o ---

THE FACTS
Distance: 14½ miles (23Km)
Grading: Rough and technical off road section
Off Road: 20%
Start/Grid Ref: Keswick, GR 270234
Maps: O.S. Outdoor Leisure 4
Grub Stops: Tea shop at Grange

--- o 0 o ---

YOUR ROUTE
Leave Keswick on the B5289 Borrowdale road. In about 2 miles (3km) look out for a road on the left which climbs steeply to Watendlath. Stop at the famous 'Ashness Bridge' to admire the view behind you. At Watendlath ride into the village over a bridge then turn right over another bridge turning left to a gate near to Watendlath Tarn. Through the gate the track splits at a signpost. Take the right fork uphill along a stony bridleway signed to Rosthwaite.

The slippery, stony climb levels out to a reasonably good track to a gate. Keep straight ahead to start the descent. This part of the route becomes technical with slippery angled rocks to unbalance you. If you do not feel confident dismount over the worst parts of the track. Another hazard presents itself on the downhill, culverts! These rather large humps and ditches across the track are negotiable with care. Ignore the right turn through the gate and continue downhill. When the track turns left at the wall slow down and go through the gate on the right. Then downhill again to the road. At the road turn right and continue along Borrowdale perhaps calling in at the Bowderstone. In about 2 miles (3km) turn left over a stone bridge to Grange. Continue along through the village and return along the quiet road around the back of Derwentwater to follow signs for your return to Keswick.

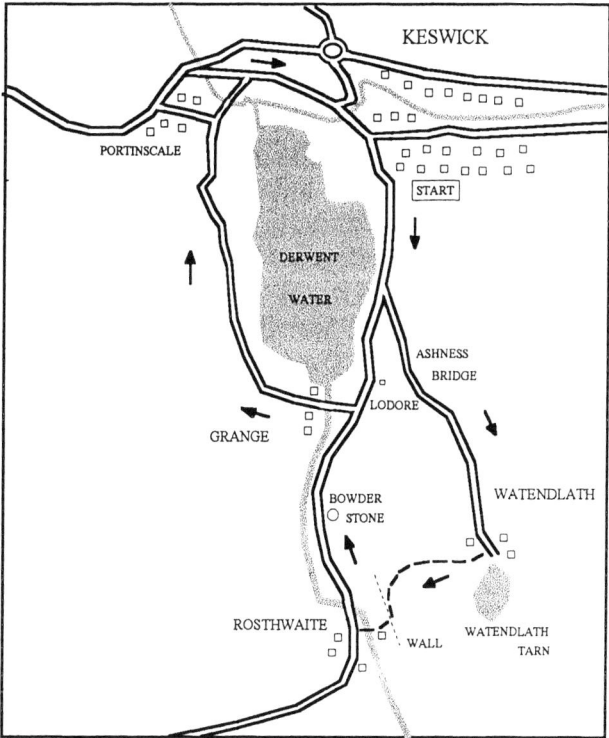

THE BORROWDALE BASH

*N**estling at the foot of the Honister pass is Seatoller. A small village with
a farm and a few cottages. A most interesting pair of cottages now form
the Yew Tree restaurant/pub. It was originally two cottages which were built
in 1628 when the Borrowdale area was alive with mining. German miners
were imported to work the copper and lead mines, they were housed on one of
the islands of Derwentwater to keep them apart from the locals. It is thought
that some miners would have lived at the cottages which is now the Yew Tree.*

*The Yew Tree is alive with memorabilia with many features of the old
cottages preserved. Old photographs bring back memories of the mining days
and one of the many interesting features is a collection of policemen's hel-
mets. This ride starts and finishes at Seatoller so you will have time to visit
the Yew Tree for some refreshment.*

- - - o O o - - -

THE FACTS
Distance: 8 miles (13km)
With road extension 19 (30km)
Grading: Moderate
Off Road: 45%
Start/Grid Ref: Seatoller, GR 245138
Maps: O.S. Outdoor Leisure 4
or O.S.Landranger 89
Grub Stops: Yew Tree at Seatoller. Cafe in Grange

- - - o O o - - -

MOUNT UP!
L eave the car park at Seatoller turning right past the Yew Tree and up the
steep hill to Honister Pass. At the top of the hill when the road flattens out
turn right along a wide track which is a bridleway. There is a bridleway sign on
a stone at the start. Follow this track as it descends to a gate and continue
along a good track for about a mile. Keep straight ahead at the fork then
descend (with care) amongst the rocks to the river below. Aim for two wooden
bridges to the left now soon bearing left past a barrier onto a wide track. At the

junction turn right to eventually arrive at Grange. If you are taking the short route back to Seatoller turn right through the village, cross the bridge then go right at the road which takes you back to Seatoller.

If you wish to take the longer route back via Keswick turn left as you leave the bridleway to take the quiet road around the back of Derwentwater. At the junction at the far end follow signs for Keswick. Return on the Borrowdale road to Seatoller.

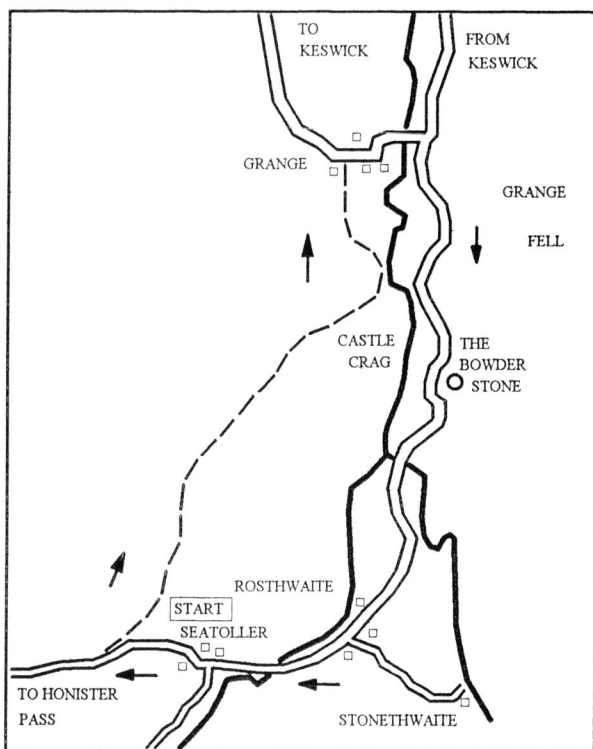

TO KESWICK

FROM KESWICK

GRANGE

GRANGE

FELL

CASTLE CRAG

THE BOWDER STONE

ROSTHWAITE

START

SEATOLLER

TO HONISTER PASS

STONETHWAITE

PEDAL POWER AT POOLEY BRIDGE

*A*n easy ride touching the start of the Roman Road called High Street. But after the first easy climb the ride falls away towards Howtown and Lake Ullswater. No summits to conquer just a peaceful pedal with scintillating views. If a long ride is required, albeit very rough in places, you could continue along past Howtown, over the Pass alongside Hallin Fell to ride to Sandwick then take the difficult bridleway to the road at Patterdale, returning on the lakeside road to Pooley Bridge. Although I have been along the route I am not giving you a route guide. If you wish to ride it take OS Outdoor Leisure number 5 and good luck! All I will tell you is that it is passable with care!*

- - - o 0 o - - -

THE FACTS
Distance: 9 miles (15km)
20 miles (32 km) if alternative route taken on return
Grading: Easy. Difficult if alternative route taken
Off Road: 50%
Start/Grid Ref: Pooley Bridge, GR 472244
Maps: O.S. Outdoor Leisure 5
Grub Stops: Choice in Pooley Bridge

- - - o 0 o - - -

YOUR ROUTE

Start from either of the two car parks at Pooley Bridge. Set off through the village past the Sun Inn and at the mini-roundabout go in the direction of Howtown. In about 500yds go straight ahead at the crossroads signed to Roe Head. Shortly pass through a gate onto the bridleway signed to Helton. After a long pull up a stony track you arrive at a crossroads. Turn right here signed to Howtown and Roman Road.

Ride along a boggy, narrow track and after a short climb arrive at a circle of stones. Turn right opposite the stones onto a wide stony track eventually reaching a small cairn. Keep to the right of the cairn onto the most prominent path then head for a wall and trees in the distance. The track soon falls to cross a small stream then climbs up to meet the wall. Keep on the wide track which varies between being stony and grassy as it starts to fall downhill. The obvious track passes the building of a reservoir on its way to another wall and follows the wall to a gate leading to a house. Please dismount as directed as you pass through the grounds of the house. In a few yards turn left through a gate following the bridleway sign. Make your way to the road and turn right to Howtown. Pass through the houses keeping right to join the road back to Pooley Bridge.

If you are going to attempt the Ullswater circular via Patterdale turn left at Howtown. If you want to enjoy the surrounding area without the hard ride to Patterdale it is worth riding to Sandwick over the Pass then returning to Howtown before cycling back to Pooley Bridge.

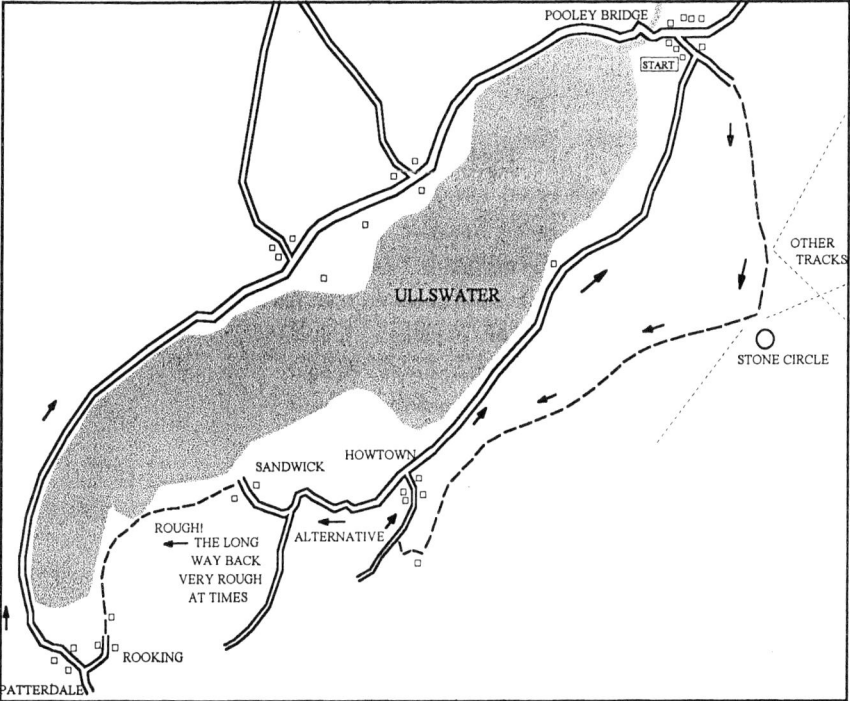

POOLEY BRIDGE

START

OTHER TRACKS

ULLSWATER

STONE CIRCLE

SANDWICK

HOWTOWN

ROUGH!
← THE LONG WAY BACK VERY ROUGH AT TIMES

ALTERNATIVE

ROOKING

PATTERDALE

THE COACH ROAD KOG KRUNCHER!

No cycling book on the Lake District would be complete without mention of the Old Coach Road which is situated between Dockray and St. John's Vale. It was for many years the superhighway of its day transporting goods and people across the windswept fells of the lake district.

For todays mountain bikers the route does present certain problems. The coach road is best ridden from the Dockray end, but getting there safely does make life difficult for cyclists. The A66! This very busy and fast trunk road has to be crossed twice and ridden along for a short way. Then a quieter A class road, the A5091 has to be negotiated. I will leave the route to you, it may be your choice to ride along the coach road then return the same way. You might like to start from Keswick, alternatively you could start from Threlkeld and risk the A66. The choice is yours!

- - - o 0 o - - -

THE FACTS
Distance: From Threlkeld 17 miles (27km)
From Keswick 25 miles (40km)
Grading: Moderate
Off Road: The coach Road is about 6 miles (9.6km) long
Start/Grid Ref: Threlkeld, GR 325255
or Keswick, GR 270235
Maps: O.S. Outdoor Leisure 5
O.S.Landranger 89
Grub Stops: Threlkeld or Keswick

- - - o 0 o - - -

YOUR ROUTE
I have drawn you a big map with suggested routes marked, I advise you to plan your preferred route using the Ordnance Survey maps and take them with you as you ride. If you decide to use the A66 route please take extreme care crossing this busy road.

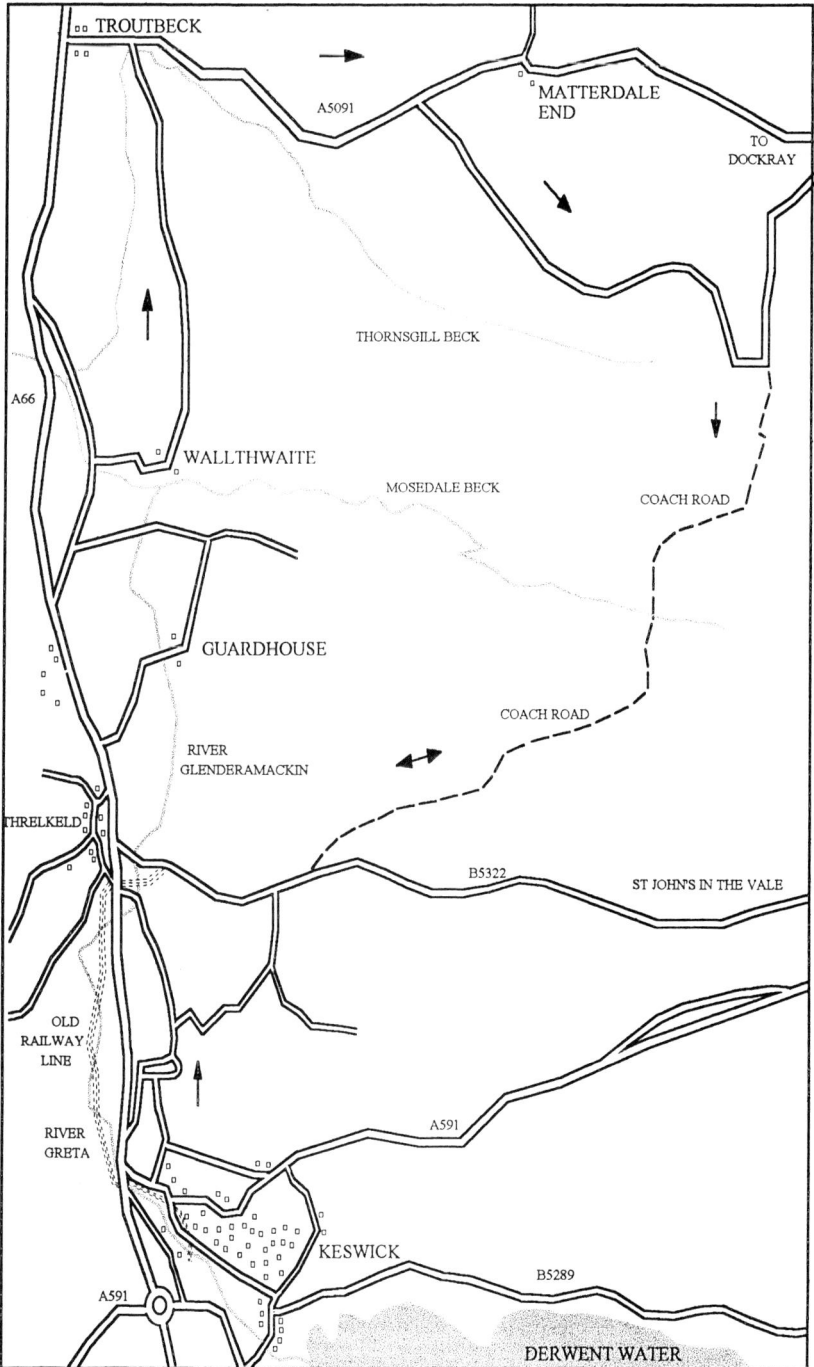

TROUTBECK

MATTERDALE END

A5091

TO DOCKRAY

THORNSGILL BECK

A66

WALLTHWAITE

MOSEDALE BECK

COACH ROAD

GUARDHOUSE

COACH ROAD

RIVER GLENDERAMACKIN

THRELKELD

B5322

ST JOHN'S IN THE VALE

OLD RAILWAY LINE

RIVER GRETA

A591

KESWICK

A591

B5289

DERWENT WATER

15

SKIDDING AROUND SKIDDAW

Skiddaw, Lonscale Fell and Blencathra tower above you as you ride around the sides of these magnificent fells on your way from Threlkeld to Bassenthwaite. However, you don't have to ride over the top of any of them as you skid around these mainly good, but testing bridleways. An option of a track across to Bassenthwaite village is suggested at the end of the ride if you have any energy left before returning on the road to Keswick. It adds three miles to the ride.

- - - o 0 o - - -

THE FACTS
Distance: 19(22) miles (30(34) km)
Grading: Moderate but exhausting
Off Road: 40%
Start/Grid Ref: Keswick, GR 270232
Maps: O.S. Landranger 90
Grub Stops: Keswick, Threlkeld and Bassenthwaite have pubs

- - - o 0 o - - -

SADDLE UP

The A66 is a very busy road. If you would like to take the quieter road past the stone circle it would be easier or you could ride along the old railway line. Whichever way you choose make your way to Threlkeld and cycle into the village bearing left towards the Blencathra Centre. Soon turn right at Blease Road. Pass the small car park and ride along the old mining track for a couple of miles. Continue along to a stile then keep to the track on the right near to a stone wall. Soon you will see Skiddaw House YHA standing on the hill in front of you which is where you are aiming for. At Skiddaw House keep almost straight ahead along a wide track which is part of the Cumbria Way. The route climbs steadily and passes between Great Calva and Little Calva on the right and Dead Crags and Cockup on the left! (*I hope the last mentioned fell isn't a bad omen!*) This leads into the downhill section to eventually join a tarmac bridleway bearing left. Soon you reach a quiet road.

If you still feel energetic you could take the bridleway opposite which is waymarked all the way to Bassenthwaite village. Leave the village to cycle to the main road where you can either take the A591 left back to Keswick or cross over the A591 and ride along the narrow road to Scarness and Bassenthwaite Lake for a while before rejoining the A591 further along.

If you don't take the option of riding the bridleway to Bassenthwaite turn left at the quiet road and in about 1½ miles join the A591 turning left to Keswick. Nearer to Keswick if the A591 is busy you might like to avoid the traffic and turn left to Milbeck, Applethwaite and Ormathwaite rejoining the A591 at the roundabout near Keswick.

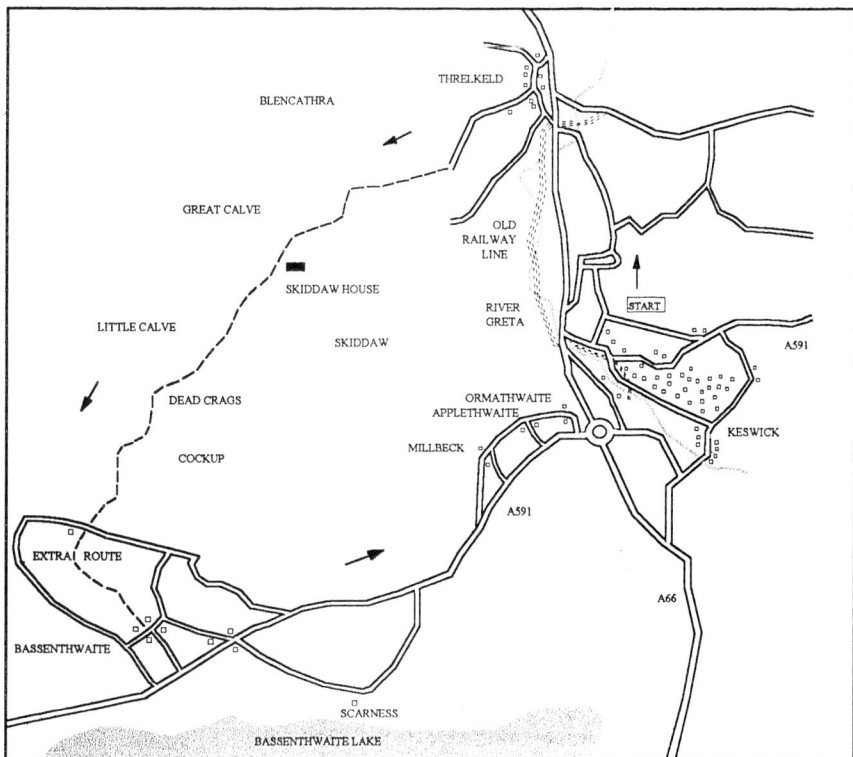

ENNERDALE END-UP!

*A*n end-up is described in my dictionary as 'to arrive by a circuitous lengthy route or process'. *Only one word is missing from the definition describing this route over Scarth Gap Pass - impossible!*

It is possible to traverse the pass with a bike but I warn you it is rough, difficult, has steps, is steep and requires a high degree of riding skill on the descent over rocks large and small down to Gatesgarth. If you are not fit and skilled and prepared to push the bike do not attempt the Pass route; instead, enjoy Ennerdale and its forest. If you do try the hard way the rewards are fantastic. The view descending from Haystacks towards Buttermere is worth all the bruises!

THE FACTS
Distance: Long route 25 miles (40km)
Short route 11 miles (17.5km)
Grading: Very rough over Scarth Gap
Easy through Ennerdale Forest
Off Road: 50% Long route, 100% short route
Start/Grid Ref: Ennerdale, GR 109154
Maps: O.S. Outdoor Leisure 4
Grub Stops: Long route, cafe at Buttermere.
Short route, ice cream trailer at Ennerdale car park

- - - o 0 o - - -

YOUR ROUTE

Start from the car park at Ennerdale forest. Head off towards the lake turning left along a wide forest road. Tarmac to start with soon turning to unmade. The ride through the forest is about five miles. At the end the road continues along to the Black Sail Hostel. It is in this area the short route finishes and you must return by the same route. The scenery is spectacular with Haycock, Steeple and Pillar prominent.

For long route riders who wish to take on the rigours of Scarth Gap Pass you must turn left before the Black Sail taking the track uphill alongside the forest. It is a long pull, the track turning right eventually to climb over the summit passing between High Crag on the left and Haystacks on the right. An old iron gate comes into view on the horizon, head for this. On the way you pass through a boggy area, look for evidence of bike tracks through the mud, it will give you encouragement to think *'you are not alone'*!

The track traverses the summit then falls steeply, some walking here I think. Head for a gap in the wall below then bear right onto a more prominent but none the less difficult track. There are some rideable parts but sudden lose stone and rocks appear without warning so please take care. Buttermere Lake soon appears and the bruises seem worth it just for the view. Continue down with a mixture of rocks and varying degrees of descent to arrive at the bottom to exit through a gate then across to the farm to exit onto the road. Left here to Buttermere for refreshment then on past Crummock Water, Loweswater through Lamplugh then following signs for Ennerdale Lake back to the car park.

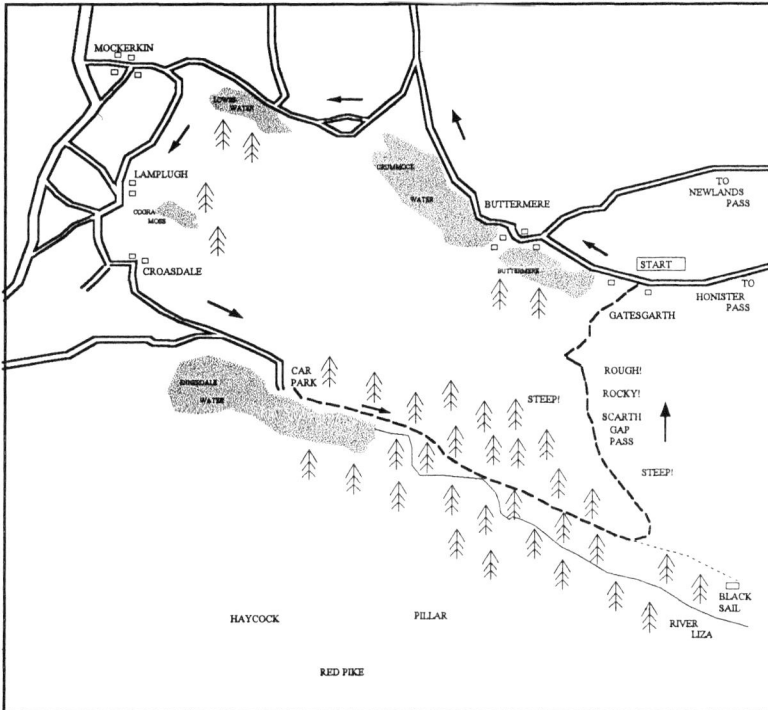

KAMIKAZE AROUND KENTMERE

The 'Kamikaze' were a group of pilots who performed suicidal missions. The similarity to Mountain Bikers is obvious as we take the bridleway to Kentmere over the Garburn Pass negotiating culverts, stone and slippery base rock. It is a challenging ride which is demanding on legs and lungs. It requires a good riding technique on both the ascent and descent. The reward is the view, which you will have plenty of time to admire as you stop for lengthy rests! The return is a bit easier once the climb up the side of Kentmere Park is achieved to cross a grassy part then downhill to the road along a wide, relatively smooth bridleway.

--- o 0 o ---

THE FACTS
Distance: 13 miles (21km)
Grading: Expert. Tough guys & gals only!
Off Road: 65%
Start/Grid Ref: Church Bridge, Troutbeck, GR 412027
Maps: O.S. Outdoor Leisure 7
Grub Stops: Take plenty of food and water with you,
there is nothing much available until it is too late!

KNEE PADS ON!

The start is near Church Bridge a couple of miles along the A592 Kirkstone Pass road from Windermere. Turn left at the bridge on the A592 over Trout Beck, you can't miss the bridge but the left turn is immediately after it. A few yards along the road there is a car park for about ten cars. Leave the car park, now under pedal power and turn right over the bridge. In a couple of hundred yards (mtrs) turn left up a steep bridleway. The hard work begins now, not only is it steep but the surface is loose. Climb all the way to the summit as the bridleway varies from loose stone, slate, grass and rock.

The view to the left across to Troutbeck and Stony Cove Pike is outstanding as is the view behind you as Lake Windermere appears. Press on ever upward to reach the summit where the track is flat through Garburn Pass to a gate for a technical descent over some dastardly rocks. The track does become smoother however and rolls downhill into Kentmere where you join the road with superb views over Kentmere and along the River Kent. Arriving at the road at Kentmere village turn left to ride downhill to the church keeping right at any doubtful junctions. At the church turn right along a bridleway signed to Kentmere Hall. At the farm (*Kentmere Hall*) turn left in front of the house through a gate with a blue waymark. Cross the beck then bear left and climb a long hill eventually passing through a gate onto grass. Follow the obvious track keeping to the wall on the left to a gate. Through the gate cross a wide beck. Leave the farmers tracks now bearing left along the beck side. When the beck bends to the left you must go right picking out the track towards two trees on a grassy knoll straight ahead. Go round the knoll bearing right following the obvious track all the way to a gate in the corner of the field on the right.

Keep straight ahead now on the worn track if a little wet at times passing through several gates to eventually reach a signpost and a wide, walled bridleway. Turn left here signed to Grassgarth. Join a quiet road at the farm and carefully ride down the narrow, twisty downhill to exit onto the busy A591 road at Ings. Go right then shortly take great care turning right again onto a quieter road to eventually reach the A592. Turn right here to return to Church Bridge.

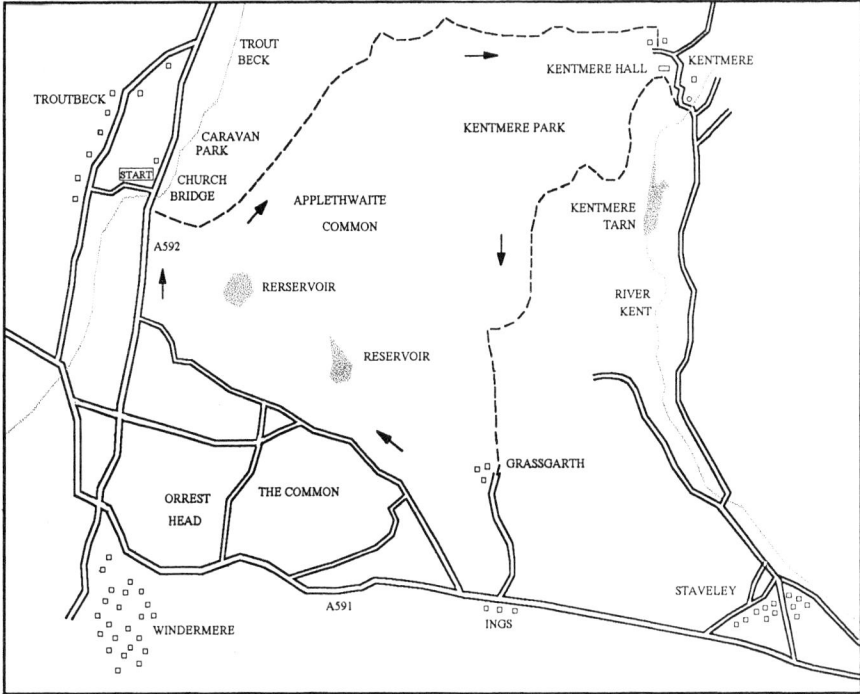

GOING BALLISTIC AROUND BUTTERMERE

*L*ake Buttermere and the adjacent Crummock Water are well away from the hustle and bustle of the popular tourist areas. Tranquil and non commercialised they represent the ideal getaway, however they are popular and having only small car parking areas an early start is advised. This route is short and easy, but a few options are thrown in for you to explore on your bike to make the ride a little more exciting and demanding.

The Fish Hotel is famous for being the home of the 'Beauty of Buttermere,' a young woman whose sad tale I will not relate here. In the church at Buttermere is a memorial to that great Lakeland walker, Alfred Wainwright.

- - - o 0 o - - -

THE FACTS
Distance: 5 miles (8km)
Extra route if required 4 miles (6.4km)
Grading: Easy
Off Road: 60%
Start/Grid Ref: Buttermere, GR 175170
Maps: O.S. Outdoor Leisure 4
or O.S. Landranger 89
Grub Stops: Two hotels and a tea shop at Buttermere

- - - o 0 o - - -

YOUR ROUTE

This route is a complete contrast to most of the routes in the book. It is for you to have a leisurely day out on a short smooth track and perhaps linger by the lake. If you feel adventurous the bridleway to Crummock Water and beyond is for you to explore, but please take a map with you.

There are lots of small car parking areas dotted around Buttermere but they soon become full, be warned! Take the road alongside the Bridge Hotel passing the Tea Shop on the way. At the Fish Hotel keep to the bridleway on the left of the Hotel and continue along this well surfaced track. Follow the path around to the right then over a bridge. The route is to the left but if you would like to explore from here turn right towards Crummock Water. The track is sometimes undefined and boggy and turns west up Scale Knott. Explore as far as you wish then return to the bridge and take the smooth path alongside the lake. Take care, this is a multi user bridleway and is sometimes used by wheelchairs. Keep on this smooth track to eventually meet the road at Gatesgarth. Turn left here along the quiet road to return to Buttermere.

- - - o 0 o - - -

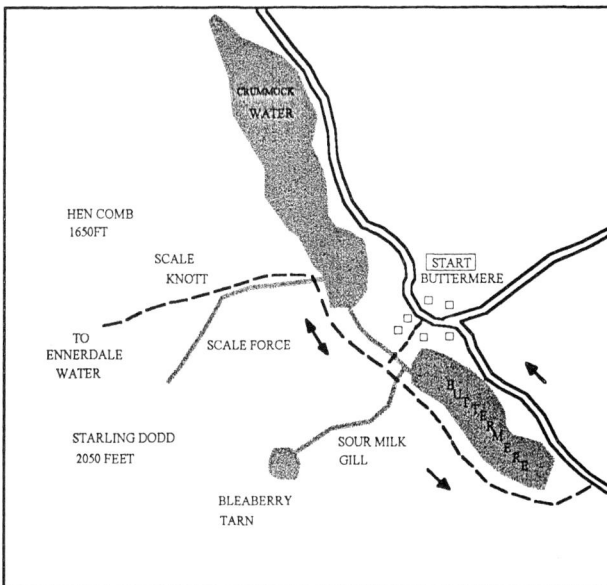

RIGHTS OF WAY

- **BRIDLEWAYS** - (Blue markings) Open to cyclist, walkers and horses.
- **BYWAYS** - (Red markings) Open to cyclists, walkers, horses and some traffic.
- **PUBLIC FOOTPATHS** - (Yellow markings) No cycling.
- **OPEN LAND** - Moorland, farmland etc. No right of access unless permission from landowner is obtained.
- **TOWPATHS** - Some are available for cycling without restriction, some are not. Others need a cycling permit available from British Waterways.
- **PAVEMENTS** - No cycling.
- **CYCLE PATHS** - Watch out for these marked paths. Information usually available from Borough and County Councils. A book containing cycle-paths in the North of England is soon to be available by the same author as this book.

CYCLING WITH SAFETY

- Prepare your cycle before riding.
- Carry spare clothing.
- Take food and water with you, even on the shortest ride.
- Always carry a good map and a compass.
- Take a whistle in case of emergency breakdown or injury.
- Always tell someone where you are going and what your expected time of return will be.
- Carry identification.
- Wear a helmet.
- Take care downhill especially off road, dismount if doubtful.
- Watch out for loose surfaces on corners.
- Learn first aid.

OTHER TRAILBLAZER BOOKS

Mountain Biking around the Yorkshire Dales
Mountain Biking the Easy Way
Mountain Biking around North Yorkshire
Mountain Biking around Ryedale, Wydale & North York Moors
Mountain Biking on the Yorkshire Wolds
Beadle's Bash - 100 mile challenge route for Mountain Bikers

Walking on the North York Moors
Walking the Ridges & Riggs of the North York Moors
Short Walks around the Yorkshire Coast
Walking to Crosses on the North York Moors
Walking to Abbeys, Castles & Churches
Walking on the Yorkshire Coast

The Crucial Guide to the Yorkshire Coast
The Crucial Guide to Ryedale and the North York Moors
The Crucial Guide to York & District
The Crucial Guide to Crosses & Stones of the North York Moors

Curious Goings on in Yorkshire